SHARPEN YOUR AX

SHARPEN YOUR AX

THE INTERCESSOR'S GUIDE TO AVOIDING BURNOUT

ALEATHEA DUPREE

Copyright © 2017 by Aleathea Dupree

In accordance with the U. S. Copyright act of 1976 as amended, and in accordance with the Digital Millennium Copyright act of 1998 as amended, the scanning, uploading, and electronic sharing of any part of this book without the permission of the publisher constitute unlawful piracy and theft of the author's intellectual property. If you would like to use material from the book (other than for review purposes), prior written permission must be obtained by contacting the publisher at permissions@aleatheadupree.com. Thank you for your support of the author's rights.

Unless otherwise noted, all Scripture quotations are from the New King James Version® (NKJV). Copyright © 1982 by Thomas Nelson, Inc. Used by permission. All rights reserved.
Scriptures noted AMP are taken from the Amplified ® Bible. Copyright © 1954, 1958, 1962, 1964, 1965, 1987 by The Lockman Foundation. Used by permission.
Scriptures noted AMPC are taken from the Amplified® Bible. Copyright © 1954, 1958, 1962, 1964, 1965, 1987 by The Lockman Foundation. Used by permission.
Scriptures noted CJB are taken from the COMPLETE JEWISH BIBLE. Copyright© 1998 by David H. Stern. All rights reserved. Used by permission.
Scriptures noted ERV are taken from the Easy to Read Version. Copyright © 1987 by World Bible Translation Center. All rights reserved.
Scriptures noted EXB are from The Expanded Bible. Copyright © 2011by Thomas Nelson, Inc. Used by permission. All rights reserved.
Scriptures noted ESV® are from The Holy Bible, English Standard Version®. Copyright © 2001 by Crossway, a publishing ministry of Good News Publishers. All rights reserved.
Scriptures noted GW are taken from GOD'S WORD®. Copyright © 1995 God's Word to the Nations. Used by permission of Baker Publishing Group.
Scriptures noted MSG are taken from THE MESSAGE. Copyright © by Eugene H. Peterson 1993, 1994, 1995, 1996, 2000, 2001, 2002. Used by permission of NavPress Publishing Group.
Scriptures noted NASB are taken from the New American Standard Bible®. Copyright © 1960, 1962, 1963, 1968, 1971, 1972, 1973, 1975, 1977, 1995 by The Lockman Foundation. Used by permission.
Scriptures noted NASBRE are taken from the New American Bible, revised edition. Copyright © 2010, 1991, 1986, 1970 Confraternity of Christian Doctrine, Washington, D.C. and are used by permission of the copyright owner. All Rights Reserved.
Scriptures noted NLV are taken from the New Life Version. Copyright © 1969 by Christian Literature International.
Scriptures noted NOG are taken from the Names of God Bible. Copyright © 2011 by Baker Publishing Group. All rights reserved.

ISBN: 097122403X
ISBN-13: 978-0971224032

This book is dedicated to

*Every intercessor and prayer warrior
called by God to stand in the gap.*

CONTENTS

Preface — ix
Introduction — 1

Chapter One
Rest — 4

Chapter Two
Sharpen Your Spiritual Senses — 18

Chapter Three
Pray with the Spirit — 31

Chapter Four
Watch Your Mouth — 41

Chapter Five
Set Boundaries — 52

Chapter Six
Divorce Yourself from Other People's Opinions — 63

Chapter Seven
Love — 71

Epilogue
Whose Intercessor Are You? — 84

PREFACE

As I sit down to write this book, I am aware that this is as much for me as it is for you. It is a much-needed reminder of the need to maintain a healthy perspective and balance between the responsibility and the privilege of prayer. Let this book serve as a bookmark in the chapters of your prayer life. Turn here often. Don't wait until you need to. Make it a part of your preemptive strategy for a successful lifestyle of prayer.

INTRODUCTION

"If the ax is dull, and one does not sharpen the edge, then he must use more strength; but wisdom brings success."

—Ecclesiastes 10:10

Prayer is like an ax. When wielded by a skilled intercessor, it is one of the most powerful means of cutting through the plans of the enemy and fulfilling God's purposes in the Earth. The usefulness of an ax is determined by how sharp it is. If an ax is used on the wrong things, at the wrong time, or in the wrong way, it will become dull. Even when used correctly, care must still be taken to maintain its sharpness. A dull ax can still be used. But the use of it will require more strength, more time, and more effort to accomplish the task. The same is true when prayer is misused, ill-timed, or mishandled. Your spiritual ax of prayer will become dull. When that happens, even if you are strong spiritually and diligent in your prayer life, if you continue using a dull ax, you will get weary, you will become less effective, and it won't be long before you're completely burned out.

God cannot effectively use burned-out intercessors. He never intended prayer to become a staggering weight. And it is not His desire to see you so frustrated and fatigued that you can't even enjoy the life He gave you. If you're reading this and you are one of those intercessors who knows what it's like to struggle under a burden of prayer, or a prayer warrior who knows what it feels like to fight tired, or the go-to prayer person that everyone else relies on to "get a prayer through," help has arrived! In the pages that follow, you will find wisdom and strategies revealed by God to refresh, regroup, and retrain His intercessors. As you employ these strategies, you will bring success to your ministry of intercession and relief to yourself.

INTRODUCTION

In each chapter, there are thought provoking questions. My recommendation is that you take the time to reflect on and answer these questions. They will help you to gauge how sharp your intercessory prayer life is. Get together with others who are involved in the ministry of prayer and discuss the content. Share your successes and failures so that others can learn from what works and avoid traps designed to drain their prayer lives. Incorporate what you learn from this book into your prayer life. And then train others to do the same.

CHAPTER 1

REST

"Come to Me, all you who labor and are heavy-laden and overburdened, and I will cause you to rest. [I will ease and relieve and refresh your souls.] Take My yoke upon you and learn of Me, for I am gentle (meek) and humble (lowly) in heart, and you will find rest (relief and ease and refreshment and recreation and blessed quiet) for your souls."
—Matthew 11:28-29, AMPC

Rest is a spiritual principle and a holistic necessity. It is a posture of stillness and quietness that is required in order to be refreshed and to receive from the Presence of the Lord. Rest is a command that is frequently disobeyed, and a discipline that is often avoided. Rest is critical to the effectiveness and longevity of the intercessor. This is a lesson I learned through an experience I had some years ago which I refer to as my "pit season." And prayer had everything to do with how that season began.

It started about six years ago. I had been burning the candle at both ends, and I was quickly burning out. At the time, I was the administrator of a nationwide intercessory prayer group called the Wall of Intercessors. This ministry was not my own idea. It was a mandate I had received from the Lord while in prayer. From its inception, the Wall grew quickly. The Lord had His hand on it, and we were receiving miraculous answers to our prayers.

As word spread about the Wall, requests came from around the world. Since I was the administrator for the group requests came to me first, and then I distributed them to the rest of the group. It was not uncommon for me to receive prayer requests that I was asked not to send to the Wall. These were requests people wanted me to pray for privately. And I did. Frequently I received requests from emergency rooms and other crisis situations. Often such requests came in the middle of the night or before dawn. During those times, I would pray through those requests on my own.

My daily prayer time was three o'clock in the morning until six or seven o'clock in the morning. But instead of spending my time fellowshipping with the Lord as I loved to do, almost all my time was spent interceding for others. Night after night and day after day this continued.

Prayer requests came via text messages, email messages, and social media. People would stop me to ask for prayer before church services began, during services, and after services. Almost everywhere I went, even at non-church related events, I was praying for people. This in and of itself was not a bad thing because I understood that the anointing is designed to attract and deal with problems. One of the main problems was that I was not taking any time to rest and refresh myself. I was so preoccupied with everyone else's requests that I failed to hear the repeated demands for rest that were coming from my own spirit, soul, and body.

I lived with an overwhelmingly pervasive feeling of exhaustion. My mind was tired. My body was tired. Even my spirit felt like it was struggling under a heavy load. From the moment I woke up in the mornings, the stream of requests would begin. I began to feel like I was alone in a crowd, surrounded by people who only sought me out when they wanted something from me. Fatigue had settled into my bones. Weariness summed up my existence, and I started to feel completely disconnected and alienated.

I was worn out physically, emotionally, and spiritually. I had poured out continually until I reached a point where my cup was empty. Unfortunately, I kept pouring. I was no longer drawing from a reservoir but draining out the last drops leaving myself completely dry. An old mentor of mine once gave me an analogy for ministering like this. He told me that when you minister, it's like pouring water out of a glass that has stones on the bottom. He went on to say that you must always replenish the water in the glass. Otherwise, the more you pour, the closer you get to the bottom, and the stones—

issues you have in your own life—become exposed. That glass was me, and I had reached a point where all my stones were exposed.

Before this time, I could discern strongholds in other people's lives and help them break free. I could walk through fire without even the smell of smoke on me. But during this pit season, my walls became so broken down that instead of breaking others free, I became vulnerable to whatever was attacking them. Depression and suicide pursued me. If it had not been for the grace of God covering me, I'm certain my life would have been destroyed.

It felt like a scream was trapped inside me somewhere between my belly and my chest. I desperately wanted to let it out, but I couldn't. I needed a safe place to bleed, but I couldn't find one. Who does the intercessor go to when she is in desperate need of prayer? Who could I trust with the level of transparency I needed to have? These were just a couple of the questions I wrestled with.

Day after day, my voice grew more silent. My prayers were replaced by songs others had written. And after a while, not even the words of the songs could speak for me anymore. Tears became my only language day and night. In the months that followed, everything that was familiar was removed. Like crutches being kicked out from under a broken leg, I lost my balance, and I slipped deeper into the pit. Like Joseph, my robe of many colors was snatched away, and I was left naked in a dark pit. All that was left was a dreadful silence.

One day, it felt like everything was crashing down around me, and I felt like I was on the verge of a nervous breakdown. I couldn't take anymore, so I literally ran out of the house, jumped into my car, and started driving. I wanted to get near a lake or river or something just to at least let my eyes drink in something serene and calming. But on the way, literally a few yards away from my intended destination, the car's steering stopped working. While I was driving, it just stopped working! I wrestled with the wheel, and somehow I managed to pull into a nearby parking lot. So much for my quest for serenity! My car broke down, and I broke down and wept. I could not escape the pit not even for a moment.

Week after week I went to church, and my pit went with me. People looked at me curiously wondering why I was no longer leading prayer every Sunday. The "prayer warrior" was benched. No one sat me down. I sat myself down because I knew that I had nothing left to give. Few had the courage to ask what was going on with me, and those who did were met only with stony silence and stifled tears. I couldn't explain to them what was happening because I couldn't explain it to myself. So, I sat in the pew and kept listening for words that might possibly form the rungs of a ladder that I could use to climb out of that dark place. I sat until even tears refused to come anymore, just a deafening solitude.

The devil had little to do with what I was going through. Yes, he was there trying to take advantage of my vulnerable state with every possible opportunity. But, I later learned that it was God who was allowing me to experience the pit. He was bringing me to the end of everything so that He could teach me lessons about prayer that I would never forget. The pit was part of a process of purification. Before I entered the pit, I thought of purification as cleansing from sinful habits and intentional acts of disobedience to God's word. It never dawned on me that my failure to rest was in God's eyes an act of disobedience and an impure habit from which I also needed to be cleansed.

I had been in the pit for months, and God had not spoken a word to me. There were times when His tangible presence would suddenly overshadow me as if to remind me that He was still there. But I was too engrossed in the darkness to respond or to appreciate His touch. The most I could do was notice. When He did speak, He told me to come away and spend time with Him. It was the first time in a long time that I heard His voice so clearly. I wasn't sure what was going to happen or what He was going to say to me. I just knew I had to get away.

I drove to a retreat center which was tucked away in the mountains of North Carolina. I arrived late on a Friday afternoon for a weekend stay. I settled in, and I waited for Him to speak. On the first full day, He didn't say anything, and neither did I. But on the next day, as if in our own private Sunday morning service, He spoke to me at length. Out of everything He said to me that day, there was one short sentence that changed my life and my attitude toward the ministry of prayer forever! "Rest is as important as prayer."

When Jesus trained His disciples in ministry, He also trained them to rest. In Mark 6 we see Jesus sending out His twelve disciples to do ministry for the first time. As soon as they returned from their ministry assignment, the first thing Jesus tells them to do is find a quiet place where they could retreat away from the people and rest. (Mark 6:30-32 GW):

> 30 The apostles gathered around Jesus. They reported to him everything they had done and taught. 31 So he said to them, "Let's go to a place where we can be alone to rest for a while." Many

people were coming and going, and Jesus and the apostles didn't even have a chance to eat. 32 So they went away in a boat to a place where they could be alone.

Do you think the timing of His instruction was a coincidence? I assure you, it was not. It was an intentional strategy and a prototype for success in ministry that Jesus modeled and expects us to follow. Notice Jesus did not only instruct them to rest but to come with Him to rest. Jesus seemed to be more, or at least as concerned about making sure His disciples rested than He was about their ministry accomplishments. Jesus supports getaways. He instructs you and I as His followers to have times when we get away from people, and go to a place where we can rest from the demands of ministry.

The scripture even goes as far as to mention that the people desiring ministry would not allow them to rest long enough even to get a bite to eat. This is something every intercessor should take to heart. People who want to receive ministry will not allow you to rest. In their times of need, they will make requests, usually without any regard for your state of well-being. You are the one responsible for being intentional about taking time to rest. As an intercessor, you might feel a sense of obligation when people ask for prayer. But you really only have one obligation as an intercessor. We'll talk more about that in a later chapter. However, taking time to get away to rest is not to be confused with abandoning your post. There is a difference between setting aside times to rest and refresh yourself and going AWOL (absent without leave). Nonetheless, rest is a spiritual principle which should not be violated or ignored. The ministry of intercession must be partnered with rest.

When God called you into the ministry of intercession, He called the whole person, spirit, soul, and body. There is a spiritual dynamic to prayer, but prayer also involves the physical body and the soul. All three should be functioning well. As powerful as your spirit and soul are, if your body is in a state of exhaustion, fatigued, or sick, it will inhibit the function of your spirit and soul. If you don't believe that the body can affect how you function as an intercessor, go to the morgue and ask any one of the corpses to pray for you. No matter how powerful you are in the spirit, if your body ceases to function properly due to lack of rest, you (that is, your spirit and soul) will cease to function properly in this earth. And so will your ministry of intercession.

Your flesh—your physical body—is not your enemy. It was created by God to house your spirit and soul. And if it is not cared for properly and dies, not even God can occupy it. A "prayer warrior" who is always tired won't do as well in warfare as a rested one. And an intercessor who is weary and worn out can't pray well.

Helping others is good. But don't make the mistake as an intercessor of prioritizing the physical, emotional, mental, and spiritual welfare of everyone except yourself. Your own welfare must be a priority. This is not selfish, it's self-preservation, and it ensures longevity and promotion in ministry. I told you that the Lord told me that rest is as important as prayer. He also told me that until I learned how to rest, He would not promote me in ministry because I would burn out. Imagine that! Your promotion can be withheld from you, not because you're not called, qualified, or anointed, but because you refuse to rest.

Ministry will wear you out if you are not intentional about getting rest. Without rest, intercession becomes hard work like using a dull ax, and prayer becomes burdensome. Your function as an intercessor on the earth is very valuable to God. But a burned-out intercessor cannot respond appropriately to God's prayer assignments. When He searches the earth for someone to stand in the gap and intercede, it is your duty to see to it that you are rested enough to respond.

Think for a moment. Are you violating the spiritual principle of rest? Rest is not merely a suggestion. It is a spiritual principle and a command (see Matthew 11:28). Rest is posturing yourself in stillness and quietness to receive from the Presence of the Lord (see Isaiah 30:15). Rest is a necessity for your body, soul, and spirit. If God who is Spirit and Jesus as a man took the time to rest, you should too (see Mark 6:31). Rest is a discipline (see 1 Thessalonians 4:11). Make it your aim to rest. Rest is a command (see Psalm 46:10). Be obedient.

CHAPTER 2

SHARPEN YOUR SPIRITUAL SENSES

"But solid food belongs to those who are of full age, that is, those who by reason of use have their senses exercised to discern both good and evil."
—Hebrews 5:14

Some years ago, I had an experience that forever changed my perspective about prayer requests. Up until that time, I assumed that God wanted me to pray for every request for prayer that I received. So, whenever I received a prayer request, I prayed. That's what an intercessor is supposed to do, isn't it? After all, who else would be sending me prayer assignments but God? The devil would never tell me to pray, right? Wrong! I learned the hard way that the devil also sends prayer requests. Do you remember the scripture that says the devil transforms himself into an angel of light (2 Corinthians 11:14)? Have you ever stopped to think how he could use that disguise to interfere with your prayer life? If you are not aware that the devil can present a request to you that seems from all appearances to be a valid prayer request, you may find yourself accepting prayer assignments that were sent straight from hell. Here's how it happened to me.

A friend and fellow intercessor contacted me one day and related what sounded like a desperate plea for help. She told me of a woman who had contacted her with a tragic story involving the death of a newborn and the devastating aftereffects. My friend asked me to join her in reaching out to this woman to provide encouragement and prayer. After hearing the heartbreaking details of the story, I naturally wanted to help. Little did I know that the story was carefully crafted bait designed to lure me into a satanic trap. And my compassion was the targeted inroad for carrying out this very strategic plan.

I accepted the assignment and began to intercede earnestly. Every time the woman and I communicated, she added more layers to her story, and each new disclosure was more heart-wrenching than the last. It got to the point where most of my prayer time was spent focused on her mounting prayer requests. It was not uncommon for her to contact me in the middle of the night while I was praying. So, I was either praying for her or communicating with her. Either way, my prayer time was being dominated.

At first, I did not realize what was happening. I just thought I was responding to what appeared to be the dire needs of another human being. I could not have been more wrong. I had been lured into prayer. And I was not the only one. Three intercessors—my friend, another intercessor, and I—were laboring in prayer for this woman and spending time communicating with her.

Suddenly, strange things began to happen to each of us. For example, on one occasion, my friend was approaching her car, and all of a sudden, she became disoriented and faint and could barely move. Up until that moment, she had been feeling perfectly well. She recognized that what was happening was a spiritual attack on her body and managed to get an urgent prayer request to me. I, along with some intercessors from the Wall immediately provided prayer reinforcement. And as we prayed, she recovered.

On another occasion, the other intercessor involved was mysteriously contacted and threatened. She did not know the person who contacted her, but somehow, she was known to the person. To substantiate the seriousness of the threat, the caller disclosed very personal information that had been discussed only between the intercessor and her husband in the confines of their home. I also experienced a spiritual attack on my health and strange occurrences around my home.

The other intercessors and I initially assumed the attacks were sent by the enemy to prevent us from praying for this person. We were wrong. We were in fact, being laid siege upon because we had opened ourselves up to the enemy by praying for a request that had been sent by him. When we accepted this demonically inspired prayer assignment, we engaged ourselves in a battle we were never supposed to have been fighting and inadvertently opened ourselves up for these attacks. In our ignorance, we had unknowingly partnered and come into agreement with the enemy, and the resulting chaos ensued.

Thankfully, the Holy Spirit began to reveal what was really happening. He let me know through various ways that I needed to stop praying for this person. (Yes, the Holy Spirit will at times direct an intercessor not to pray.) His message was loud and clear. But, by this time, because I had been continually pouring out of my soul in prayer on this woman's behalf, I was so emotionally invested that I found myself struggling to walk away. An intercessory soul tie had developed.

What is an intercessory soul tie? An intercessory soul tie is a spiritual bond that is created when you join yourself to another person in prayer. I strengthened the bond by praying consistently and intently for her over time. The only thing that broke this soul tie was my obedience to the voice of the Holy Spirit. I did not obey His instruction the first time I heard it or even the second time. But the third time, He urged me emphatically and urgently to "Leave it alone!" I stopped praying for her, cut off all further contact, and shifted my attention back to other prayer requests. As soon as I did this, the attacks stopped.

To show you how committed and vigilant the enemy was in keeping me entangled in this prayer assignment, when I stopped praying, the woman immediately contacted me to find out why I was no longer praying and to encourage me to continue. How did she know I was no longer praying? I had made no announcement to her or anyone else. She knew because, like it or not, she and I had a spiritual connection. She even told me she could feel it when I prayed, which would explain why she could feel it when I stopped praying. My prayer activity was being monitored by demonic informants in her life. The enemy's goal was to keep me distracted with his prayer requests, because as long as I focused on his assignment, I was not focused on God's assignment.

Why did it take God speaking to me three times for me to hear and obey His voice concerning a prayer assignment, but it only took the enemy speaking once for me to get involved? The Lord gave me the answer to that question some time afterward. He spoke to me specifically concerning intercessors. This is what He said. "My children are dull of hearing. I am speaking and have spoken, but My children aren't paying attention to Me. They are more tuned in to what the enemy is saying or to what the soulish man is saying." Is His statement true of you? I invite you to take a moment and think about how you've been praying. Whose voice is directing your intercessory assignments? Have you accepted a prayer request you should have denied or ignored?

If I had taken the time to consult the Holy Spirit and paid attention to what He had to say, He would have told me from the start not to accept this prayer request. It might seem incredible to believe that God would tell an intercessor not to pray for someone. But He does do that. And I would not have been the first intercessor to receive such an instruction.

In Jeremiah 14:11 (NABRE), the Lord tells Jeremiah not to pray for the people:

> Then the Lord said to me: *do not intercede* [emphasis added] for the well-being of this people.

This is proof that it is possible for an intercessor to pray for someone and that prayer would go directly against the will of God.

On another occasion in Acts 8, a man named Simon witnessed the apostles laying hands on people and praying for them to receive the Holy Spirit. He wanted to be able to do what the apostles were doing. So he asked the apostles to lay hands on him and pray for him. He did not receive prayer. Instead, he received a rebuke and a curse. Then Simon specifically asks for prayer that the things which the apostle had spoken against him would not happen (Acts 8:24). Again, we have no record of this prayer request being addressed.

In as much as God has given intercessors the power to pray, not every prayer request qualifies for the resource of prayer. In short, God does not want us praying for every prayer request that we receive. Some requests should be rejected or completely ignored. Therefore, it is important to find out from God what He wants you to do. And hearing what He has to say requires the use of your spiritual senses.

Hebrews 5:14 teaches us that strong meat belongs to the spiritually mature, whose spiritual senses are trained through practice to be able to discern between good and evil. Some prayer requests are evil, but they are not presented that way. They will come to you as something good; an "angel of light" hiding behind the guise of what looks like a valid need, a compassionate concern, or an earnest desire for what appears to be right. People have prayer requests. God has prayer requests. And the devil also has prayer requests. We have to be able to discern the difference. Sharp spiritual senses are able to discern between good and evil, and that includes good and evil prayer requests. If you are unable to make that distinction, you may find yourself trying to tackle strong meat with milk teeth. In other words, you may find yourself taking on prayer assignments that you're not supposed to be involved with and fighting battles that you were never meant to fight.

God speaks. If you don't hear His voice, it's not because He is not speaking. It is likely because you have not yet sharpened your spiritual senses enough to hear or understand His voice. To think that God always speaks using words that we can hear is a misconception. He does not. It is up to God to choose how He wants to communicate. It is up to us to hear His voice regardless of the method He chooses to use. That is why practicing using our spiritual senses is so important. Sometimes the word of God is not audible, it is visual, or in some other sensory form. Habakkuk 2:1 says, "I will ... watch to see what He will say to me," not listen to hear what He will say. Sometimes the voice of God is felt. God can communicate with you through any of your spiritual senses. Just as you have five physical senses, you have at least five spiritual senses: hearing, touch, taste, smell, and sight. God can use any of these mediums to communicate with you. He can use images, visions, dreams, fragrances, sensations, hearing, even taste or activity in your mouth as well as spoken words.

Prayer is in the spiritual dimension. Therefore, to function effectively in that dimension, we must use our spiritual senses. Before and as you pray, engage and use your spiritual senses. What are you hearing, seeing, tasting, smelling, feeling? So often when we receive prayer requests, we are so preoccupied with what man is communicating to us, that we fail to find out what God is communicating to us through our spiritual senses. Before and as you pray, pause and pay attention to what the Holy Spirit is communicating to you. Becoming skillful in the use of your spiritual senses will not happen automatically. You have to practice. The Holy Spirit will help you in this endeavor. He is the Master Trainer who can help all of us to further develop our spiritual senses if we so desire.

Have you ever read Daniel 7:25? It reveals a strategy of the adversary to "wear out the saints of the Most High." One of the ways he attempts to wear out intercessors is by sending wrong prayer requests. If you are not spiritually discerning, you will wear yourself out laboring in prayer over requests that are designed to tie up your time and to distract you from where your focus needs to be.

Intercessors are being worn out not because they are praying. They are being worn out because they are accepting wrong prayer assignments. Some people, like Simon in Acts 8, don't need prayer, they need a word or a rebuke. Sometimes, as we saw in Jeremiah's case, prayer needs to be denied. Only one with sharp spiritual senses will be able to know how to respond accordingly to each prayer request. Remember that the devil also sends prayer requests. And if you're not careful, your prayer time may be spent distracted by things the devil has brought your way through people who appear to be in need.

Again, I encourage you to take a moment and think about how your prayer time has been spent lately. On whose behalf have you been spending most of your time praying? Where did those assignments come from? Whose voice has taken priority in your prayer life? Is it God's voice or someone else's? Has your prayer time been consumed battling with the enemy on someone else's behalf? Are you praying about God's requests? If you find yourself becoming worn out because of your prayer assignments, it is likely the devil rather than God directing your prayer life.

CHAPTER 3

PRAY WITH THE SPIRIT

"It is like this: No one knows the thoughts that another person has. Only the person's spirit that lives inside knows those thoughts. It is the same with God. No one knows God's thoughts except God's Spirit."
—1 Corinthians 2:11, ERV

Many intercessors have become skilled in praying in the Spirit, but there are not as many who are skilled in praying *with* the Spirit. And there is a difference. You can be praying in the Spirit and still not be praying with the Spirit. It's an issue of whose agenda is driving your prayer life. Allow me to explain.

The Holy Spirit is our Prayer Partner. Most of us readily accept Him as our Prayer Partner when it comes to helping us to pray most effectively. But being a prayer partner is a relationship that works both ways. On the one hand, the Holy

Spirit prays with you concerning the requests that are on your mind, whether they be your own or the requests of others. On the other hand, there are times when He wants you to pray with Him about the requests that are on God's mind.

From ancient times until now, God has made it known that there are times when He looks for someone to pray with Him about His own requests. For example, in Genesis 18, the wickedness of Sodom and Gomorrah was so great that God came down to personally meet with Abraham and provide an opportunity for him to make intercession. God knew that Abraham understood His personality which is why He trusted Him to pray about His concern. Abraham understood that God was righteous and that even in light of the wicked dealings in Sodom and Gomorrah, He desired to show mercy (see verse 25). So, God took the time to wait while Abraham joined with Him as a prayer partner and interceded. A God who is altogether holy, righteous, and just needed an intercessor to stand in the gap so that He could show mercy instead of wrath. This was God's personal prayer request.

Again, in Ezekiel 22, there were things happening in the land that invited God's wrath. But God, who desires mercy rather than judgment, searched for someone who would intercede on His behalf so that His wrath could be averted. This prayer request was not initiated by the people. It was initiated by God. He wanted to spare the people the consuming fire of His wrath. But He needed an intercessor to come into agreement with Him and pray concerning what He desired to do.

As I previously stated, there are three sources from which we can receive prayer requests. Prayer requests can come from people (including ourselves), from the devil, and from God. In the previous chapter, I discussed the need for us as intercessors to have our spiritual senses sharpened so that we can recognize requests that originate from ungodly sources or for ungodly purposes (that is, purposes that are not supported or desired by God). Conversely, we also need to be able to recognize when prayer requests do come from God.

One of the ways you can recognize a God-initiated prayer request is when the Holy Spirit invites you to pray. Such an invitation may be presented in a variety of ways. Here is one of them. Have you ever been going about your day and suddenly the words from the Spirit begin to bubble up inside you prompting you to pray? That's an invitation, not just to pray in the Spirit, but to pray *with* the Spirit. It's God's prayer request. But unless you are spiritually sensitive and aware of it, you may dismiss it and miss an opportunity to pray with the Spirit about something that is on the mind of God.

This is how I was introduced to praying with the Spirit. Some years ago, I had what I call a God thought. This is the term I use for original thoughts that I recognize as being initiated by the Holy Spirit. The thought was for me to spend some time each day in prayer. There was nothing remarkable or original about that. But it was the thought that followed that captured my attention. This time of prayer was not to be spent praying for my own requests or the requests people had sent to me. This time was especially for praying with the Holy Spirit about whatever requests or concerns He wanted to pray about. And that's what I started to do. I would find a comfortable and quiet place, let Him know that I was ready to pray for whatever He desired, then I would pray in the Spirit.

Sometimes I would pray for a short while, sometimes longer depending on how He led me. Sometimes His concerns were made known to me. Most of the time, they were not. It didn't matter. All that mattered was that, by faith, I availed myself to Him for His prayer requests. Initially, I set aside a specific time to do this each day. In doing so, I established His requests as a priority in prayer, and I became more sensitive to His promptings to pray. After some time, my availability was no longer dictated by a set time on the clock. I availed myself to pray with Him at any time He so desired.

In 1 Thessalonians 5:19, we are admonished, "Do not quench the Spirit." Other translations say that we should not suppress, subdue, or be unresponsive to the workings of the Spirit. When the Holy Spirit invites you to partner with Him concerning His prayer requests, it is an invitation that should not be ignored. There is a reason why He is prompting you to pray. And there is a reason why He has selected you in particular to pray.

The Holy Spirit is our Helper. And every intercessor needs His help and lots of it! We may receive many prayer requests, but the reality is, we don't know what or how to pray for any of them without His help. There is another reality to consider, and that is, we are His helpers. We help Him to pray! The Bible says that we are God's coworkers (1 Corinthians 3:9). He works with us, and we also work with Him. There is a necessary interdependence that takes place in intercession. You need God to pray with you, and He needs you to pray with Him.

God still searches for intercessors. But sometimes, His intercessors are so busy praying for everyone else's requests that God's requests go unnoticed or ignored. One of the ways burnout occurs in the life of an intercessor is by ignoring God's prayer requests and taking on everybody else's. When this happens, intercession becomes a burden.

Matthew 11:29-30 (AMPC) says:

> Take My yoke upon you and learn of Me, for I am gentle (meek) and humble (lowly) in heart, and you will find rest (relief and ease and refreshment and recreation and blessed quiet) for your souls. 30 For My yoke is wholesome (useful, [good—not harsh, hard, sharp, or pressing, but comfortable, gracious, and pleasant), and My burden is light *and* easy to be borne.

If you find yourself becoming weary and burdened in your ministry of intercession, be assured that burden didn't come from God, because His burden is "light and easy to be borne." 1 Corinthians 9:7 (CJB) says, "Did you ever hear of a solider paying his own expenses?" If you're enlisted in the army, you don't have to bring your own bullets. If you are interceding and find yourself becoming worn out, somewhere along the line, you started using your own bullets or resources to get the job done. That is not what God wants for you. If He has given you an assignment, He will provide everything you need to get the job done in a wholesome way.

Intercession is a divine assignment. You are employed by God to fulfill His vision. As intercessors, our foremost responsibility is not to pray for the requests that are initiated by people, but to pray with the Spirit about the requests that are on God's heart. Generals don't receive orders from privates. That means, our orders should be coming from God and His requests should take top priority. Those requests may come directly from God or through select people, and we must be able to discern who those people are. But above all, we should always remember that we are God's intercessors, not man's.

There is a verse of scripture that is one of the most painful verses in the Bible for me to read. It's found in Isaiah 59. In that passage, God saw that there was no justice in the land. Then in Isaiah 59:16a (AMPC), it says this:

> And He saw that there was no man and wondered that there was no intercessor [no one to intervene on behalf of truth and right]

That verse pains me for two reasons. First, God had to look for an intercessor. He needed someone to partner with Him in prayer, and He had to look to see if an intercessor was available. God, the creator of the intercessory job description and the One who employs and equips every intercessor had to search for one! That's an indictment all on its own! But the part that brings tears to my eyes is knowing that not only were His intercessors missing in action, but God himself *wondered* because of it. Think about that for a moment. God wondered! That word that is translated *wonder* means that God was *shocked, amazed, awestruck, astonished, stunned, appalled* that no intercessor was found! It was, for lack of a better word, unbelievable to Him! God had an expectation that was unmet, a desire that went unfulfilled. And only an intercessor could have satisfied His request.

When people have prayer requests, they can find you. But when God has a prayer request, can He find you? Can God count on you to pray with Him, or does He have to look for you? And if He does, will He be shocked, stunned, and appalled as a result? Can God visit you at any time to make known His prayer requests and trust you to intercede? I invite you to pause for a moment and think about the following question. When was the last time you asked God what He wanted to pray about? I encourage you to reconsecrate yourself to God as His intercessor. Make it a goal to be sensitive to His requests and to give them priority above every other person's prayer request. Your mission is to fulfill God's purposes, not man's. That is His primary reason for calling you into the ministry of intercession. And your Prayer Partner is counting on you to pray with Him to that end.

CHAPTER 4

WATCH YOUR MOUTH

"Out of the same mouth come both blessing and cursing. These things, my brothers, should not be this way [for we have a moral obligation to speak in a manner that reflects our fear of God and profound respect for His precepts]."
—James 3:10, AMP

The mouth of an intercessor is not an ordinary mouth. It is a mouth that is anointed as God's mouthpiece on the earth. The mouth of an intercessor is not for swear words, gossip, coarse jokes, idle, vain or empty words which will grieve your Prayer Partner, the Holy Spirit. Ephesians 4:29-30 (AMPC) says:

> 29 Let no foul *or* polluting language, *nor* evil word *nor* unwholesome *or* worthless talk [ever] come out of your mouth, but only such [speech] as is good *and* beneficial to the spiritual progress of others, as is fitting to the need *and* the occasion, that it may be a blessing *and* give

grace (God's favor) to those who hear it. 30 And do not grieve the Holy Spirit of God [do not offend or vex or sadden Him], by Whom you were sealed (marked, branded as God's own, secured) for the day of redemption (of final deliverance through Christ from evil and the consequences of sin).

How can you effectively pray with your Prayer Partner, the Holy Spirit, with the same mouth that is being used to offend, vex or sadden Him? This kind of disharmony with the Holy Spirit does not lend itself to agreement in prayer. Therefore, the mouth of an intercessor should be consecrated for prayer. When you realize that you are God's intercessor, and as you pray in and with the Spirit, you will come to understand that when you speak, you speak as God's representative in the earth.

> Whoever speaks, is to do so as one who is speaking the utterances of God; whoever serves is to do so as one who is serving by the strength which God supplies; so that in all things God may be glorified through Jesus Christ, to whom

belongs the glory and dominion forever and ever. Amen. (1 Peter 4:11, NASB)

Complaining, gossiping, and other evil communication cannot coexist with effective prayer. When you speak idle, empty, vain, or evil words, it's like throwing water on the same wood that you want to use to build a fire. Your mouth should be kept pure so that God can speak through it at any time. Cursing, gossip, slander, coarse jokes, harsh words, complaining and overall negative speaking are just a few of the obvious ways that the mouth of an intercessor can become defiled. But I want us to focus on two ways that may not be as obvious but are just as effective in dulling the edge of your prayer life.

Two of the most powerful words we can employ as intercessors are 'Jesus' and 'Amen.' Our 'Amen' brings us into agreement with the Word of God which is our most powerful weapon. It seals our declarations of God's principles and His promises which are the very foundation of our prayers. And the name Jesus is the only name given that brings heaven, earth, and everything under the earth to its knees in submission to the authority of God. It is through the Name of Jesus that we wield authority over everything that is not like God. Yet, these two powerful words are two of the most trivialized words in the mouths of many intercessors.

Our 'Amen' is a sacred reminder to a covenant keeping God. And the Name of Jesus is the holiest name we can utter. In the New Testament, one common translation for the word mouth is the edge of a sword. When we reduce our 'Amen' and the Name of Jesus to mere clichés or minced oaths, we place, as it were, a sheath over the swords of our mouths and dull the edge. As a result, what should be a fatal blow to the plans of the enemy becomes not much more than a mild prod.

'Amen' and the Name of Jesus are not words that we should use lightly. When we unleash our 'Amen' and the Name of Jesus, we should always make the connection to what these words really mean and represent. Otherwise, they become as empty, idle words in our mouths. Words spoken that are devoid of authority are tantamount to intercessory suicide. You may not even realize this has happened until you come face to face in an enemy confrontation. This is what happened to David.

I met David in college. He was a believer, very involved in ministry, and an all-around nice guy. One day, David, a group of my college mates, and I were sitting around talking. He shared an experience he had one day on his way home from campus. It went like this.

David was on a bus headed home and noticed a woman who he perceived to be demon possessed. When he arrived at his stop and exited the bus, the woman followed him shouting all kinds of obscenities behind him. At first, he tried to ignore her thinking she might leave him alone or go in a different direction. She did not. Finally, when he couldn't take it any longer, he turned around and rebuked her in the Name of Jesus. To his surprise, the demon rebuked him and told him that he had no right to use that Name because he had used it too carelessly too many times in the past. The demon may have been calling David's bluff, so to speak, to challenge his authority. But there was enough truth in what the demon said about how he had used the Name of Jesus to cause David to retreat in fear and defeat. The Name of Jesus still had all the authority and power it ever had, but David was unable to wield that authority with confidence in that confrontation. It was a lesson I've never forgotten. I hope you will never forget either.

We end our prayers with 'Amen.' as a declaration of certainty that we have prayed the will of God, and He has heard and responded to our requests. Yet many have trivialized their amen by using it to punctuate everyday commonplace speaking. 'Jesus' should not be used as a minced oath that we use in place of an expletive or otherwise profane expression. It is the name of the Most Holy One given to us so that we can function on His behalf with His authority in the earth. We cannot use His name vainly and expect to get results in prayer. Honoring the Name of Jesus and being conscious of the power of our 'Amen' makes us sharp in prayer.

A name is representative of the character of the person. When you pray in the Name of Jesus, your goal should be to pray in His character also. Failure to realize this goal will minimize your effectiveness in prayer. Your character and the proper development of it is extremely important. Character is more important than how many Bible verses you know, how long you pray, how much you speak in tongues, how anointed you are, or what title or credentials precede or follow your name. Godly character is everything! If you are beginning to recognize your need to develop your character but you're wondering where to begin, a good starting point is being mindful of your words.

Before we can pray in the character of Jesus, there is something we must do first. It is found in 2 Chronicles 7:14, a verse of scripture that intercessors are famous for quoting. It reads:

> If My people who are called by My name will humble themselves, and pray and seek My face, and turn from their wicked ways, then I will hear

from heaven, and will forgive their sin and heal their land.

This verse is a call to action for intercessors. I have heard many preachers, teachers, and speakers talk about the "humble themselves" portion of the verse. And for the most part, intercessors don't (or shouldn't) mind the "and pray and seek My face" portion of the verse. The part that is most avoided is the portion that says, "and turn from their wicked ways." God wants the hearts of His people, especially His intercessors, to turn away from "their wicked ways" and do things the way He wants us to do them. This is the prerequisite and preface for the remainder of the verse.

We need individual repentance and a commitment to purity and holiness so that when we pray, the power of God can be released unhindered to deal with whatever needs to be dealt with. Individual repentance and a commitment to holy living is where intercession should start. God needs people who are clean vessels who will seek His face and receive instructions for strategic prayer. Until God's intercessors repent individually, we may pray, but we will not see the kind of impactful changes He wants to effect in the Earth.

It is to your advantage to be mindful of what you say before prayer. Be mindful also of what you say after prayer. What you say after prayer is as important as what you say during prayer. Negative speaking and doubt-filled words will put the brakes on the dynamic ability of right words that have been released in prayer. It is our responsibility to be careful with our words so that we don't undermine our prayer lives in our daily conversations.

God's house is supposed to be a house of prayer. This refers to the physical building where we gather corporately. But more importantly, it refers to us. We are His house. Our bodies are His temple. And just as the brick-and-mortar structure of a physical building that has been dedicated to God and the vessels therein are to be consecrated as holy unto God, we too, as His vessels are deemed holy and should be consecrated for God's use. That is why in Romans 12:1 (AMPC) Paul says:

> I appeal to you therefore, brethren, *and* beg of you in view of [all] the mercies of God, to make a decisive dedication of your bodies [presenting all your members and faculties] as a living sacrifice, holy (devoted, consecrated) and well pleasing to God, which is your reasonable (rational, intelligent) service *and* spiritual worship.

A decisive dedication of your body to God, including and especially your mouth, is an intentional act. God will not do this for you. You are responsible for using your members along with their faculties or capabilities in ways that please God. That means, the way you use your mouth and the words it is capable of producing should please God.

God is a God of truth. Everything He does is based on truth. Psalm 22:4 says, "For the word of the LORD is right, and all His works is done in truth." In order to effectively communicate with Him, the language He understands and responds to is truth. And in order to communicate for Him most effectively, your words must also be right, and your works must also be done in truth. The words you speak in intercession and in conversation should be meaningful, purposeful, intentional, making tremendous power available. This happens when both the source of those words and the vessel carrying and expressing them are pure. This is what makes us useful to God for His work:

> The Lord wants to use you for special purposes, so make yourself clean from all evil. Then you will be holy, and the Master can use you. You will be ready for any good work. (2 Timothy 2:21, ERV)

Consider for a moment how you have been using your mouth. Have you made a decisive dedication of your mouth and manner of speaking to God? If you haven't, I encourage you not to delay another moment. Make a decisive dedication of your mouth and words to God. Do it now.

CHAPTER 5

SET BOUNDARIES

"We are allowed to do all things [all things are lawful/permissible], but not all things are ·good for us to do [profitable; beneficial]."
—1 Corinthians 10:23, EXB

When I was in my early twenties, I read a book called "Boundaries" by Henry Cloud and John Townsend. The subtitle of the book says everything about why I needed it: "When to Say Yes, How to Say No to Take Control of Your Life." I had serious boundaries issues, particularly when it came to saying no to others. I was an expert in sacrificing my own well-being and the peace of my own soul on the altar of being unwilling to offend someone else. And as a result, I suffered. Reading the "Boundaries" book was the first practical step to bringing my self-inflicted suffering to an end.

Not long after I completed the book, I had the opportunity to attend a Boundaries seminar that was being held a few hours away from where I lived. It was a life-changing weekend! I finally learned why and how to say, "No!" When I returned home, I immediately started putting my newfound "No" into circulation. At first, it was extremely difficult saying no to people who had been so accustomed to me always saying yes to their every request. People were offended, at times even indignant, claiming their perceived right to continue receiving positive responses to what they considered undeniable requests. But the more I practiced saying no, the easier it became.

Unfortunately, when I started to minister in intercessory prayer, I did not always keep my boundaries intact. If someone asked me to pray, I did. It didn't matter who made the request, what the request was for, what time the request came, or what I was doing at the time. Morning, noon, night, middle of the night, before the break of day, I prayed for every request. I used to carry my phone around like a pager, responding to every ring and vibration. Eventually, I learned that it's not my job (or yours) to always be on call for every request. God is the only one who is always available. He is the only one who never sleeps. He doesn't need to. You do!

As was mentioned in the chapter about rest, the anointing is designed to attract and deal with problems. But the anointing is also designed to give you the power to say no when you need to. Allow me to explain. Ecclesiastes 10:1 (MEV) says:

> A dead fly causes a stench in mixed anointing oil, so a little folly is more weighty than wisdom and honor.

Oil represents the anointing. As a God-appointed intercessor, you should recognize and be aware that you are anointed to do what you do. The oil on your life attracts problems because the oil on your life carries solutions. However, you should also recognize that the same oil is designed to keep "flies" from contaminating the anointing on your life.

The devil is also known as *Beelzebub* which means *lord of the flies*. His job as Beelzebub is to contaminate the anointing on your life by tempting you to make foolish decisions rather than wise and honorable ones. Sometimes, that "fly" or temptation comes in the form of a prayer request to which you need to say "No!" If you're anything like me, as an intercessor, you feel more than an unction to pray. You feel a responsibility. But if wisdom is not exercised, you may find yourself praying for situations and people that you should have walked away from. It might seem selfish and maybe even a little cruel to consider saying no to someone who asks you to pray for him or her. It is not. It is wisdom.

A wise decision is the best fly swatter. It is unwise to make decisions like a checker player, jumping at every prayer request that's in front of you. Make decisions like a chess player, anticipating the consequences multiple moves in advance. Only the Holy Spirit can give you this kind of insight and foresight, and He is willing to give it to you if you ask. I encourage you to ask, because the anointing is too expensive to let one bad move cost you everything.

If we are not careful, we can step over the boundary line of intercession into enabling others in their dysfunction, immaturity, and co-dependency. This is why it is so important for us to be led by the Spirit. The Bible has already admonished us that there is a way that seems right to a person, but the end of that way leads to death (see Proverbs 14:12). Death is not always physical. You can experience the death of your focus; the death of your peace; the death of your assignment; the death of a relationship; as well as the death of your physical health.

Some of the same people you labor over in prayer who reject the word of God, walk in disobedience, and are content to remain in their dysfunction or childish spiritual state would be the main ones crying over your casket after you've worn yourself out and prayed yourself into an early grave. Boundaries will keep you out of a casket. Don't be afraid to say no. Just because you receive a prayer request doesn't mean it's supposed to be your prayer assignment.

As an intercessor, your assignment may require you to be a watchman on the wall. Psalm 127:1 says, "Except the Lord builds the house, they labor in vain who build it; except the Lord keeps the city, the watchman wakes but in vain." If the watchman "wakes," that implies that the watchman also takes time to sleep! Your personal phone was never meant to be a 24-hours a day prayer hotline. In other words, you should not always be on call. There are times when you should express your "No." by turning off your phone and going to sleep or doing something other than praying.

You might wonder how you should respond if the prayer request is related to a life-or-death situation. If you are prepared spiritually and physically to handle the request and you are led to pray, by all means pray. It is important to note that when you are correctly aligned spiritually, prayer does not always have to be long or require exhausting effort.

Another thing to remember is that the same mouth that asked you to pray can also be used to pray to God. There are times when you should allow the other person to pray as you come into agreement. Wisdom and the leading of the Holy Spirit will dictate the most appropriate response. The bottom line is, prayer is not a resource reserved exclusively for intercessors. Every believer has access to God's throne of grace where mercy and grace to help in time of need are readily available (see Hebrews 4:16).

If we would be completely honest with ourselves, some of us would have to admit that we enjoy it when people always come to us with their prayer requests. It makes us feel important and powerful. (I'll talk more about this in the next chapter.) But it is essential that we maintain dependency on and partner with the Holy Spirit in prayer, and encourage others to do the same. The Holy Spirit is the ever-present Prayer Partner, not you. Allow the Holy Spirit to help you and direct your path in prayer. Proverbs 3:5-8 (MSG) says:

> Trust God from the bottom of your heart; don't try to figure out everything on your own. Listen for God's voice in everything you do, everywhere you go; he's the one who will keep you on track. Don't assume that you know it all. Run to God! Run from evil! Your body will glow with health, your very bones will vibrate with life!

If we want to maintain a wholesome prayer-life balance, we must be sensitive to the leading of the Holy Spirit and maintain dependence on Him. I implore you to be obedient to Him when He cautions you not to pray for someone. It may be that there is something He is trying to work out in that person's life and your constant prayerful intervention may be getting in the way.

Prayer is not always the answer to an individual's problem. Sometimes, necessary action on their part, not yours, is what is required. This applies particularly in the case of those who bring prayer requests to you over and over and over again. When that happens, that is indicative of a two-fold problem: yours and theirs. Theirs because they continue to demand of you what they at some point should be doing for themselves. And yours because you allow it to continue. All believing men and women are supposed to pray, not just you. If you are referred to by anyone as their personal prayer warrior, it may sound like a compliment, but it may be an indication that you are failing in the areas of boundaries.

One of the most crucial times you should say no is when you know your cup is drained. If you are constantly pouring out on behalf of others, your cup will eventually get drained. And If you know your cup is drained, don't do as I did and try to pour when you know your cup is empty. Take time to rest, refresh, and refuel. Saying no does not mean abandoning your post. It means not allowing man's priorities to reassign you to a different post. Stay true to your assignment. And as you pour out, take the time to allow the Master to fill you up and turn your water into wine so that when you next pour, others will get the very best out of you. Unless and until that is possible, just say, "No!"

Another reason you should put your "No!" into action is so that you can develop intimacy with the Lord, whose intercessor you are. Intercession is birthed out of intimacy. When you get close to God, you'll get to know Him; He'll share His heart with you; you'll become sensitive to His voice and moods; you'll start to understand His priorities. Intimacy with the Lord is a critical component of your prayer life. But, how can you develop intimacy with Him if you're always praying for someone else? Taking the time to prayer for others is important, but taking the time to develop intimacy with the Lord is absolutely essential!

Your "No." could be the most loving and wise response to someone's request for prayer. There is a type of person I refer to as a "professional counselee." This the kind of person who constantly bombards you with requests (often the same ones over and over). It would be more profitable to such a person and to you as an intercessor if you redirected the requests instead of always handling them yourself. It is not wise and it can be very draining to position yourself as the one who always has the answers. An intercessor at best should be a pointer to the One who really does have all the answers. So, I encourage you to take the 'S' off your chest! You are not the Savior, and the world will not stop if you say "No."

There are ways you can tactfully and graciously communicate your "No." without actually using the word no. Keep in mind that for some people, especially those who feel a sense of entitlement, graciousness and tact may not work. In such instances, an unequivocal "No." should get the job done.

Do you have your "No." ready? If not, take the time to think of ways you can graciously but firmly say no. Be preemptive in your preparation. Otherwise, you may yield to the pressure of the moment when a request is presented to you and respond rashly. Keep your "No." on standby and be ready to use it. Sooner or later, you'll need it!

CHAPTER 6

DIVORCE YOURSELF FROM OTHER PEOPLE'S OPINIONS

"They were more concerned about what people thought of them than about what God thought of them."
–John 12:43, NOG

Pride is an insidious enemy of every intercessor. It is subtle in its approach, and lethal in its effect. Pride is the lie we believe about ourselves. And if we are not careful, pride can motivate us to cater to the expectations of people when we pray.

One of the things you should be careful to guard yourself against is the praise of people. This is particularly true if you are an intercessor who is often in the spotlight as I was. There was a time when I would open every Sunday service with prayer. I had gained the reputation of being a "prayer warrior," someone who (in some people's estimation) would pray with fervor. People would often come to me and tell me how I was a "fire starter," "atmosphere shifter," "hell shaker," and such. By God's grace, I never believed the hype. But I did take note of what people were saying, and I started to realize that whenever I got up to pray, people expected me to pray a certain way. At times, I was tempted to meet that expectation. But I was determined not to fall into the trap of pleasing people. And you should be too.

We can learn an important lesson from the prophet Elijah. He experienced a visitation from God on Mount Sinai. We can find the account in I Kings 19:11-13 which says:

> Then He said, "Go out, and stand on the mountain before the Lord." And behold, the Lord passed by, and a great and strong wind tore into the mountains and broke the rocks in pieces before the Lord, *but* the Lord *was* not in the wind; and after the wind an earthquake, *but* the Lord *was* not in the earthquake; 12 and after the earthquake a fire, *but* the Lord *was* not in the fire; and after the fire a still small voice. 13 So it was, when Elijah heard *it,* that he wrapped his

face in his mantle and went out and stood in the entrance of the cave.

During this visitation, God gave Elijah (and us) a revelation of His power. All power belongs to God, and if He so chooses, He can demonstrate His power in awe-inspiring ways. There are times as we pray, the power of God may manifest through us in such ways and it stirs the souls of the people. But that should neither be our goal nor our focus. Our focus should not be on manifesting the mighty wind, the great shaking, or the roaring fire. Our focus should be on hearing the still small voice. That speaks of intimate relationship with God. Intimacy, not demonstration of power, should be the number one priority of the intercessor.

People can easily be emotionally manipulated through prayer, especially when that prayer sounds a certain way that meets their expectations. The less spiritually mature can be moved on a purely soulish level that leads them to believe that the person praying or the prayer being prayed is powerful. This is a deception.

There is another trap that every intercessor should avoid, and that is judging the quality of your prayer based on the response of the people. Sometimes, you may pray the perfect will of God and get very little response or none at all. That does not make your prayer any less impactful. When you pray, it is not important how people respond to you. It is important how God responds to you. The response of people may vacillate depending on any number of variables: mood, time of day, respect for the person praying, etcetera. And the praise of men is fickle at best. How people respond to you as you pray, whether it be praise or indifference, should never be the focus of your prayer. Your focus should be to stand before the people and say what God wants you to say, however He wants you to say it. There are times when that may look and sound like an earthquake, or wind, or fire. And there are times when that may look and sound like a still small voice. A person with an intimate relationship with God can speak two words that may sound like a "still small voice" and tremendous power can be released. It is God's prerogative—not yours and not the people's—to decide how He chooses to manifest His presence and His power.

Beware of the lie that leads you to believe that you have to pray "powerful" prayers to please people. The Bible tells us in Psalm 62:11 that all power belongs to God. Therefore, pray with the understanding that it is God who is powerful, not your prayers. Your goal should not be to pray "powerful" prayers. Your goal should be to become intimately acquainted with the God who has all power. James 5:16 (AMP) says, "The earnest (heartfelt, continued) prayer of a righteous man makes tremendous power available [dynamic in its working]." What makes your prayer powerful is your ability to be heard by an all-powerful God with whom you have an intimate relationship.

Therefore, the goal and priority of every intercessor should be to spend quality time with God in private so that when you pray in public, you pray from relationship with God and not reputation with man. Quality time is not only about spending hours and hours praying to God. It is about interacting with Him throughout your day, not only to make requests, but simply to enjoy His company.

When we become preoccupied with how we appear to people, God has nothing to do with that. That preoccupation is driven by fear. The caution that was given to Jeremiah is also the caution that we should heed. In Jeremiah 1:4-19, we see the call and assignment of Jeremiah as a prophet. He was to proclaim God's word, intent, and desire to the people to which he was sent. As intercessors, we have a similar assignment. God knew that Jeremiah (and you and I) would be concerned about how the people would respond to him (and us). This is why, in verse 8, God said:

> "Do not be afraid of their faces, for I *am* with you to deliver you," says the Lord.

And again, in verse 17:

> "Therefore prepare yourself and arise, And speak to them all that I command you. Do not

be dismayed before their faces, lest I dismay you before them."

There is something more important than the fear of people, and that is the fear of the Lord. Notice what the Lord said at the end of verse 17, *lest I dismay you before them*. God wants us to be concerned about Him and what He wants us to do more than we are concerned about the "faces" of the people. If we are afraid of being "dismayed before their faces," we should be more afraid of God dismaying us before them.

Take an honest evaluation of yourself. When you pray with or in front of people, do you find yourself thinking about how you look, or how you sound, or how "powerful" your prayer or the effect of it seems to the people? If so, you may have fallen into the people-pleasing trap of performance prayer. How much of your prayer is superficial soul-stirring fluff? Do you feel your prayer is just as effective when it is communicated through a "still small voice" as it is when it is communicated with "wind," "earthquakes," or "fire?" How much of your prayer time is spent getting to know God? If all of your prayer time is spent talking to God about other people's problems, your priorities are misplaced. Give priority to just being with Him and enjoying His presence. Divorce yourself from other people's opinions. It doesn't matter what other people think about how you pray. It only matters what God thinks about how you pray. Resist the temptation to conform your prayers to the expectations of people. And just in case it's on your to-do list, never try to impress people with "powerful" prayers.

CHAPTER 7

LOVE

"God's love has been abundantly poured out within our hearts through the Holy Spirit who was given to us."
—Romans 5:5, AMP

The dullest prayer life is the one in which love is not the motivation. God is Love. And the Spirit of God is the Spirit of Love. The Holy Spirit fills us with the love of God, makes us aware of the love of God, and brings forth or manifests the love of God through us.

Love is the essence of the language of prayer. Without love, prayer becomes irrelevant and useless. 1 Corinthians 13:1-2 (AMPC) says:

> 1 If I [can] speak in the tongues of men and [even] of angels, but have not love (that reasoning, intentional, spiritual devotion such

> as is inspired by God's love for and in us), I am only a noisy gong or a clanging cymbal. 2 And if I have prophetic powers (the gift of interpreting the divine will and purpose), and understand all the secret truths and mysteries and possess all knowledge, and if I have [sufficient] faith so that I can remove mountains, but have not love (God's love in me) I am nothing (a useless nobody).

If the love of God is not working in you, you may pray, but your prayers will not be much more than an unpleasant and disturbing sound. You may have faith, but without God's love effectually working in your life, your faith will not work the way God designed it to work. Galatians 5:6 (AMPC) says,

> For [if we are] in Christ Jesus, neither circumcision nor uncircumcision counts for anything, but only faith activated *and* energized *and* expressed *and* working through love.

Faith is the engine in the vehicle of prayer, and love is the oil. Do you know what happens when you try to run an engine that has no oil? It seizes instantly! What should be moving becomes jammed and stuck and the engine will fail. This is what happens when the engine of faith is not lubricated with the oil of God's love. Without the flow of love, faith and consequently, the prayer of faith cannot be activated, energized, expressed, or work. All believers, but especially God's intercessors, should make every effort to maintain a lifestyle that is governed by love, allowing the Spirit of Love to influence everything we do. If love has not been your motive for intercession, you have not yet successfully interceded.

Recently, my husband and I experienced a problem with our car. We were driving along enjoying a beautiful sunny day, when suddenly the alert sound started chiming. The warning message displayed on the console indicated that the engine was overheating and we should stop driving. Simultaneously, the engine power was reduced and we started to move at a crawl. My husband pulled the car over, switched the engine off, and allowed it to cool down. After some time had passed, he started the engine and tried driving the car. We had barely moved a tenth of a mile when the same thing happened again.

This time, an additional warning message was displayed indicating that the engine oil had been degraded. We realized that to continue to try to drive the car in this condition might completely damage the engine. The car was towed to a repair facility and after some diagnostics had been performed, the problem (a failed water pump) was found and repaired.

Fortunately, even though the engine had overheated, because we had promptly responded to the alert messages, the engine was undamaged. When the console message warned us about the engine oil being degraded, we assumed that the oil level was low. However, the supply of oil was not the problem. We found out there was enough oil present for optimal engine performance. But, the water pump problem was hindering the oil from working with the engine as it should.

Just as it is good practice to routinely check the oil level for a physical engine, it is wise to routinely check your "love level" to make sure the love of God is flowing through your life as it should. As long as the Holy Spirit is present, lack of love will never be the issue. He supplies love to you in abundance. But without regular spiritual maintenance, you may knowingly or unknowingly allow contaminants to degrade the performance of God's love in you and inhibit the flow of God's love through you. When was the last time you ran some diagnostics on your life? Have you checked to see if the "oil" of love is lubricating your prayer life?

The following passage from 1 Corinthians 13:4-8 (AMPC) can be used to gauge how freely the love of God is flowing through you:

> 4 Love endures long *and* is patient and kind; love never is envious *nor* boils over with jealousy, is not boastful *or* vainglorious, does not display itself haughtily. 5 It is not conceited (arrogant and inflated with pride); it is not rude (unmannerly) *and* does not act unbecomingly. Love (God's love in us) does not insist on its own rights *or* its own way, *for* it is not self-seeking; it is not touchy *or* fretful *or* resentful; it takes no account of the evil done to it [it pays no attention to a suffered wrong]. 6 It does not rejoice at

injustice *and* unrighteousness, but rejoices when right *and* truth prevail. 7 Love bears up under anything *and* everything that comes, is ever ready to believe the best of every person, its hopes are fadeless under all circumstances, and it endures everything [without weakening]. 8 Love never fails [never fades out or becomes obsolete or comes to an end].

From time to time, I review this scripture as part of my routine spiritual maintenance. If reading a particular portion of the passage makes me feel uncomfortable, challenged, or convicted, I take that as my alert message indicating a problem area that I need to address. You will also benefit from incorporating this passage as part of your own routine spiritual maintenance. Then you will be able to detect any problems and ensure that no harmful contaminants have been allowed to degrade the performance of God's love in you.

One of the most harmful contaminants and hindrances to the flow of God's love through you is unforgiveness. Love forgives.

And forgiveness is required for effective prayer. Mark 11:25 (AMPC) says:

> And whenever you stand praying, if you have anything against anyone, forgive him and let it drop (leave it, let it go), in order that your Father Who is in heaven may also forgive you your [own] failings and shortcomings and let them drop.

Unforgiveness is an issue of the heart. Refusing to forgive is disobedience to God and therefore sin. Furthermore, when you hold unforgiveness in your heart, that sin will hinder your prayer life. The word *hinder* means: *to create difficulties for someone or something resulting in delay or obstruction.*[1] There is no greater hindrance to prayer than not being heard. Psalm 66:18 (NLV) says:

> The Lord will not hear me if I hold on to sin in my heart.

It is clear to see how such a hindrance would nullify your intercessory efforts. If you pray and you are not heard, your intercession is useless! This is why it is essential for you to make every effort to rid yourself of any obstacle that keeps you from freely loving others. Dealing with unforgiveness should be at the top of that list.

Forgiveness is a choice. Like love, it has little to do with how you feel. It's a decision that you make that allows the Spirit of Love to partner with you without restriction or interference. Forgiveness is a command not a suggestion. It is not optional. It is mandatory. Ephesians 4:30-32 (AMPC) says:

> 30 And do not grieve the Holy Spirit of God [do not offend or vex or sadden Him], by Whom you were sealed (marked, branded as God's own, secured) for the day of redemption (of final deliverance through Christ from evil and the consequences of sin). 31 Let all bitterness and indignation and wrath (passion, rage, bad temper) and resentment (anger, animosity) and quarreling (brawling, clamor, contention) and slander (evil-speaking, abusive or blasphemous language) be banished from you, with all malice (spite, ill will, or baseness of any kind). 32 And

become useful and helpful and kind to one another, tenderhearted (compassionate, understanding, loving-hearted), *forgiving one another [readily and freely], as God in Christ forgave you* [emphasis added].

Forgiving "as God" means forgiving in the same way as God. So, if God, of His own volition, chooses to readily and freely forgive, we must follow His example.

Forgiveness is at the core of salvation. When Christ died on the cross, He died for all of your sins: past, present, and future. He also died for the sins of anyone who has offended you in the past, anyone who is offending you now, and anyone who will offend you in the future. Forgiveness has been made available for all. And your prayers are heard on the basis of that forgiveness. We see this in Matthew 6:14-15 where it says:

> 14 For if you forgive men their trespasses, your heavenly Father will also forgive you. 15 But *if you do not forgive men their trespasses, neither will your Father forgive your trespasses* [emphasis added].

When you refuse to forgive, you stand between the forgiveness of the cross and your offenders denying them the opportunity to receive that forgiveness. In doing so, you are in effect declaring that the forgiveness that Jesus effectuated on the cross does not work for the person who offended you. The resulting consequence is that if what Jesus did on the cross to bring forgiveness doesn't work for the person who offended you, it doesn't work for you either. This is what is meant when the scripture says if you do not forgive, you also cannot be forgiven (see verse 15). Choosing to withhold forgiveness, is choosing to embrace bitterness. Bitterness is unforgiveness with no expiration date. And the only thing that can uproot bitterness from your heart is yielding to the influence of the Spirit of Love and forgiving your offender.

God's love poured out in you transcends an emotional feeling. It is a limitless resource that you can intentionally be aware of and from which you can perpetually draw. You don't have to feel anything in order for God's love to be operating in you. This is how you can pray earnestly for a person for whom you do not feel any particularly overwhelming affection and still be operating in love. In the same way, you can deny a person's prayer request (which might feel like an unloving thing to do) and still love that person. God's unconditional love in you enables you to do what's in the best interest of another person in spite of how you feel.

Think carefully for a moment. Is there anyone who you have not forgiven? Before you rush to give an answer, you may want to ask the Holy Spirit to search your heart and reveal any unforgiveness that may be lurking there. If He shows you that there is an offense which you have not yet forgiven, address it immediately. Make the decision to forgive. The following prayer may be used to guide you through the verbalization of your commitment to that decision:

> *Father, thank you for the shed Blood of Jesus Christ, for You said in Your word, without the shedding of His Blood, there is no forgiveness of sins (Hebrews 9:22). I receive forgiveness for my sins, sins that I committed intentionally*

and unintentionally; sins that I committed by doing wrong, and sins that I committed by not doing what is right; sins that I committed willfully; and sins that I planned to commit. You said, if I confess my sin—come into agreement with You about what You say about my sin—You are faithful and just to forgive me of all my sin and to cleanse me from all unrighteousness (1 John 1:9). Because You have forgiven my sin debt, I also release those who have wronged me, harmed me, offended me in any way. You said, anyone whose sins I forgive, they are forgiven (John 20:23). I forgive their sins. Heal me of any wounds their offense may have caused. You are my Shepherd. Restore my soul. Heal me until the memory of their wrongdoings does not hurt me anymore. Heal me until the desire for revenge is purged out of my heart. Heal me until I no longer have any expectation of them to make amends for their past wrongdoings. Heal me until every hole in my soul is closed and the Love You have poured out in my heart can flow freely, even to those who have done me wrong. Thank You for the Holy Spirit who will help me through this and enable me to do this. In Jesus' Name. Amen.

Before I close this chapter, I want to briefly revisit my pit season experience. That was an experience I never want you to have. That was the experience that was in large part the catalyst God used for the writing of this book. As I neared the end of my pit season, and I started to hear God speaking again, He spoke to me often about only two things. One was rest, which I have discussed in the first chapter. The other thing He spoke to me about was love. As a burned-out intercessor, these were the two primary areas that He chose to focus on in my life. I do not believe that was by coincidence. Neither do I believe that these two priorities are unique to me. They are for each and every intercessor. Without the intentional activation of these two things, rest and love, your intercessory prayer life will grind to a screeching halt.

[1] "hinder." *Oxford American College Dictionary*. G.P. Putnam's Sons, 2002. Web. 15 August 2017.

EPILOGUE

WHOSE INTERCESSOR ARE YOU?

In a court of law, one must be authorized, appointed, and summoned to speak on behalf of the person represented. As an intercessor, you are divinely appointed to be God's intercessor on Earth. Though your prayers benefit mankind, you represent God. You speak on His behalf. And your prayers are for the fulfillment of His desires and mandates. This awareness should help every intercessor to clarify his or her assignments. Instead of intercessory assignments being dictated by individual prayer requests from people, our assignments should be driven first and foremost by what God wants to accomplish. This prioritization requires us to develop enough spiritual sensitivity to be able to distinguish between requests that are sent by God and those that are not. Once such a distinction has been made, we then need to embrace God's agenda and methodology even it means the rejection of all others. To put it more succinctly, do what God wants God's way. This is the key to avoiding burnout.

What would happen if a legal advocate (an attorney for example), regardless of expertise, current caseload, or type of case, tried to represent every individual that came to him or her with a potential case? Ineffectiveness, frustration, lack of focus, and physical and mental exhaustion are a few likely outcomes. Yet, there are intercessors who try to function in this way. They welcome a continuous stream of prayer requests around the clock attempting to single-handedly intercede on everyone's behalf. As a result, such intercessors become prey for the enemy, and get so worn out that they become useless to others, themselves, and most importantly, God.

God has appointed specific people in the earth to carry out the ministry of intercession in specific areas, for specific cases. As an intercessor, you have been appointed as a divine advocate. That does not mean that you are supposed to represent every case. On the contrary, a God-appointed intercessor is not assigned to every case, neither should he or she attempt to take on every prayer request. Each intercessor should represent the case that has been assigned to him or her. And it is God, not an earthly requester, who should determine the intercessory caseload.

Intercession is a divine assignment. There is one Employer, and He is not a man. As an intercessor, your obligations are defined by God. Everything else is optional. God goes through the trouble of searching through the earth just to find an intercessor. If He has found and appointed you, let it not be that you are so burned out with man's requests that you cannot respond to His.

THANK YOU FOR READING!

This book could not be successful without you! Please:

1. **Leave a review** on Amazon.com. Your feedback is valuable to the author and to other readers.

2. **Tell others** about the book and let them know how they can get their own copy on Amazon.com.

3. **Share what you've learned** with others who are involved in the ministry of prayer; discuss the content; train others.

4. **Get involved!** Join the Sharpen Your Ax Intercessors Network and/or get information about hosting a Sharpen Your Ax Prayer Clinic. Visit aleatheadupree.com for more info.

Thank you for helping to equip and empower intercessors everywhere and for helping to make "Sharpen Your Ax" a success!

ALEATHEA DUPREE

Author. Edifier. Faith Catalyst. Philanthropist.

"I write so that you won't hurt."

Connect with Aleathea!
aleatheadupree.com
Facebook.com/AuthorAleatheaDupree
Follow on Instagram @AleatheaDupree

Use hashtag #sharpenyourax

OTHER BOOKS BY ALEATHEA DUPREE

THOUGH THE VISION TARRY
Waiting for My Promised Mate

End your frustration. Avoid regret.
Understand why you're still waiting.

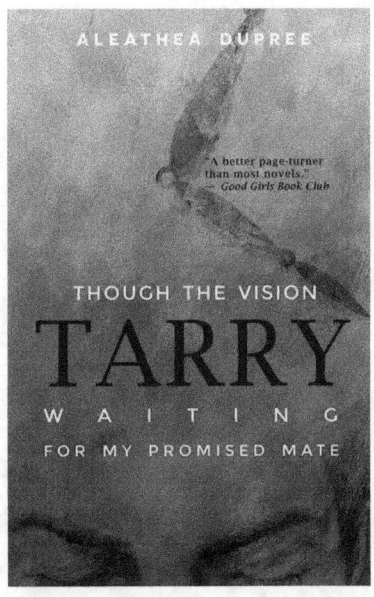

Though The Vision Tarry: Waiting For My Promised Mate addresses the frustration, anxiety, and hopelessness many feel while they're waiting on God to fulfill a promise. This transparent and compelling story helps you understand why God makes you wait and serves as a powerful reminder that God is faithful to bring His promise to pass, no matter how long it takes.

Like us at Facebook.com/WhyWait
Available on Amazon.com

CHEER UP YOUR WIFE
A DIY Biblical Guide

*** Discover God's #1 strategy
for a happy divorce-proof marriage!***

Wives come with care instructions. The problem is, most men don't know where to find them, or they don't understand them. The result? Unhappy wives. Unhappy lives. God wants you to have a happy marriage, and He has provided a solution to the problem. *Cheer Up Your Wife* gives you the easy-to-read version of a wife's care instructions and supplies all the tools you need to repair, build, or maintain a happy divorce-proof marriage!

Like us: Facebook.com/CheerUpYourWife
Available on Amazon.com

RHINO FAITH
365 Truths to Charge Ahead in Your Faith

Move your faith from "anemic" to aggressive and charge ahead!

Rhino Faith guides you day by day and step by step through the exhausting terrain of your faith journey. You will no longer suffer from "anemic" faith that is weak, tires easily, and is deficient of what it needs to produce the results you desire. Instead, you will develop an aggressive faith that will charge ahead, overcome every obstacle, and bring fulfillment to the desires of your heart.

Like us: Facebook.com/RhinoFaithBook

ALL BOOKS AVAILABLE AT AMAZON.COM

www.ingramcontent.com/pod-product-compliance
Lightning Source LLC
LaVergne TN
LVHW051508070426
835507LV00022B/3000